A **TRUE** BOOK™

# The Virginia Colony

KEVIN CUNNINGHAM

**Children's Press®**
An Imprint of Scholastic Inc.
New York  Toronto  London  Auckland  Sydney
Mexico City  New Delhi  Hong Kong
Danbury, Connecticut

**Content Consultant**
Jeffrey Kaja, PhD
Associate Professor of History
California State University, Northridge

Library of Congress Cataloging-in-Publication Data

Cunningham, Kevin, 1966–
  The Virginia Colony/Kevin Cunningham.
     p. cm.—(A true book)
  Includes bibliographical references and index.
  ISBN-13: 978-0-531-25399-1 (lib. bdg.)          ISBN-13: 978-0-531-26612-0 (pbk.)
  ISBN-10: 0-531-25399-1 (lib. bdg.)              ISBN-10: 0-531-26612-0 (pbk.)
  1. Virginia—History—Colonial period, ca. 1600–1775—Juvenile
literature. I. Title. II. Series.
  F229.C96 2012
  975.5'02—dc22                                   2011011428

All rights reserved. Published in 2012 by Children's Press, an imprint of Scholastic Inc.
Printed in China 62
SCHOLASTIC, CHILDREN'S PRESS, A TRUE BOOK, and associated logos are trademarks and/or registered trademarks of Scholastic Inc.
1 2 3 4 5 6 7 8 9 10 R 21 20 19 18 17 16 15 14 13 12

# Find the Truth!

**Everything** you are about to read is true *except* for one of the sentences on this page.

Which one is **TRUE**?

**T or F** George Washington fought in the French and Indian War.

**T or F** Jamestown was a successful colony from its beginning.

Find the answers in this book.

# Contents

**Continental army
soldier**

4

# THE **BIG** TRUTH!

**Thomas Jefferson**

# Virginia's Founding Fathers

How did the Virginia Declaration of Rights
influence other important documents? . . . . . . . . . . . . . . **36**

Patrick Henry was
one of the finest
speakers in the
colonies.

# Timeline of Virginia Colony History

**Around 10,000 B.C.E.**

Native peoples inhabit present-day Virginia.

**1607**

The colony of Jamestown is founded.

**1781**

The British surrender at Yorktown.

**1788**

Virginia approves the U.S. Constitution.

# CHAPTER 1

# Virginia's Native Americans

The area that became Virginia was home to many Native American peoples in the early 1600s. Inland groups included the Monacan and Tutelo. The Catawba and Cheroenhaka lived to the south and northwest. The Nanticoke and the Powhatan lived closer to the Atlantic Coast. They spoke Algonquian languages. These languages were related to those spoken by peoples who lived in what we now call New England.

The Powhatan and other Virginia Algonquian peoples lived in villages built near farm fields. Families lived in longhouses. Longhouses were tunnel-shaped buildings made of mats of bark or woven reeds placed over a wooden frame. The women cared for the longhouse. They also cared for the maize (corn), beans, and squash that were grown in the fields. They gathered wild plants such as berries in warm weather. Women also treated animal skins. The skins were made into clothing.

**Corn was an important crop for many of America's native peoples.**

The earliest native people arrived in Virginia between 10,000 and 12,000 years ago

**Spear fishing took a great deal of skill and practice.**

Men hunted deer and turkeys with bows. Fathers taught their sons hunting skills. Young boys practiced hunting small animals. Young girls helped their mothers. Natives living along rivers or coasts fished with short spears, nets, and wooden traps. Many peoples fished from canoes made of hollowed-out tree trunks. Oysters and clams were also food sources for the natives.

Original
13 Colonies

Area
enlarged

PENNSYLVANIA

0    miles    100

0    km    100

MARYLAND

*Potomac River*

*Ohio River Valley*

*Shenandoah R.*

Mount Vernon

MONACAN

Fredericksburg

Charlottesville

*Chesapeake Bay*

POWHATAN

*Appalachian Mountains*

TUTELO

*James River*

Richmond

Williamsburg

VIRGINIA

Jamestown

Yorktown

*Blue Ridge Mountains*

CHEROKEE

Newport News

NOTTOWAY

Norfolk

CATAWBA

*Roanoke Island*

NORTH CAROLINA

*Pamlico Sound*

*Cape Hatteras*

SOUTH CAROLINA

ATLANTIC OCEAN

Colonial boundaries

Present boundaries

GEORGIA

# The Settlers

Native Americans living near the Blue Ridge Mountains may have encountered Europeans in the early 1540s. Spanish explorer Hernando de Soto passed through the region at that time in search of gold. Peoples further east, in the Powhatan **Confederacy**, met a different group of Spaniards who took away a Powhatan boy. It is likely that some heard rumors of English settlements set up on the North Carolina coast in the 1580s.

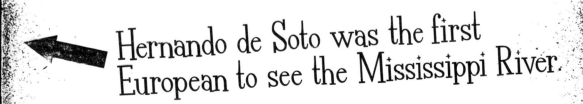

Hernando de Soto was the first European to see the Mississippi River.

**The earliest settlers came to Virginia to make money.**

# The Virginia Company

King James I of England gave the Virginia Company permission to start a colony in North America in 1606. The settlers of the colony were part of the company. Their job would be to search for gold and to farm, cut lumber, or do whatever work the company considered important. The Virginia Company's goal was to make money. The settlers would receive a share of the company's profits in return for their work.

# A Miserable Adventure

The Virginia Company sent three ships from England with settlers to begin the new colony. All 104 settlers were male. They arrived on the eastern coast of North America and sailed 60 miles (97 kilometers) up the waterway they named the James River. The settlers built a fort that would become the colony of Jamestown in 1607. Two years of misery followed. The unhealthy water at the site sickened and killed many colonists. Disease-carrying mosquitoes swarmed in summer.

Jamestown was the first permanent colony the English built in North America.

**Just over a hundred colonists helped to build Jamestown.**

Many of the men in the group belonged to wealthy families. They had joined to find gold. They tried and failed to grow corn. They had to rely on local Native Americans for food. But the colonists threatened and attacked the native people instead of dealing with them fairly. The colony's leader was John Smith. The tense relationship with the natives was eased somewhat when settler Smith began to trade with them.

**John Smith helped make peace with the native people.**

Pocahontas later married another Englishman named John Rolfe. ➡️

Pocahontas' actions helped to keep peace between the colonists and the natives.

## The Powhatan Confederacy

Many Native Americans belonged to the Powhatan Confederacy. This powerful group of about 30 Algonquian peoples numbered between 14,000 and 24,000 people. Smith met a young Powhatan woman named Pocahontas on a trading journey in 1607. Legend says she saved his life. This began a very brief period of peace between the native people and the settlers. Smith returned to England in 1609 when he injured his leg. The colony's population numbered about 500 to 600 people at the time.

The state of Delaware is named after De La Warr.

De La Warr arrived in Jamestown on June 10, 1610.

## Lord De La Warr

Jamestown's second year was as bad as the first. The Powhatan trapped the settlers inside their fort after they attacked the Indians for food. The settlers spent the winter starving and freezing. Only 60 of them remained alive when a new leader arrived with more colonists in the spring. The leader was named Lord De La Warr. His strict rules forbade misbehavior and forced everyone to work. Life at Jamestown remained challenging. But the colony began to grow.

# Tobacco

The Virginia Company had yet to make a profit. The Native Americans had no gold. The settlers kept dying. But colonist John Rolfe brought tobacco seeds from the Caribbean in 1612. The company finally had a way of making money. Jamestown shipped 2,500 pounds (1,135 kilograms) of tobacco to England a few years later. Rolfe married Pocahontas in 1614. This brought another short peace between the English and the Powhatan.

**Tobacco became an important crop for the Jamestown settlers.**

# New Way of Government

The Virginia Company faced pressure to make profits. It changed some of its rules in 1619. It allowed settlers to own land. This meant farmers actually worked for themselves. It also put a **legislature** called the General Assembly in charge. The assembly consisted of a governor and his council chosen by the company. It also included a House of Burgesses with representatives elected by the colonists. Only white males who owned land could vote.

**The new government excluded everyone except for white, land-owning men.**

There were 22 members of the original Virginia House of Burgesses.

# Opechancanough

The Powhatan chief Opechancanough (oh-pech-un-KAH-noh) became the new leader of the Powhatan Confederacy in 1618. Opechancanough had disliked how the settlers claimed Powhatan land and threatened his people. He carried out attacks in 1622 that killed 347 colonists. The English responded by killing Native Americans and destroying their villages. The war ended when colonists killed 200 native leaders with poisoned wine at a meeting to make peace. Opechancanough survived to fight 20 more years.

The problems in Virginia convinced King James to make it a royal colony under government control beginning in 1624. But new problems arose with new settlers. They farmed on the western frontier because the best tobacco-growing land was taken. The owners of large farms called plantations ran the government. They put high taxes on western farmers. They also refused to help fight off Native American attacks. A 1676 rebellion finally forced the General Assembly to treat the westerners more fairly.

A man named Nathaniel Bacon led the 1676 rebellion.

**Settlers spread farther into North America as they searched for new land.**

The assembly encouraged new settlers from Germany, Northern Ireland, Sweden, and other countries to come to the colony in the 1700s. The newcomers cleared the forests of the Shenandoah Valley for their farmland. It had previously been a Native American hunting ground. Virginians crossed over the Appalachian Mountains and into French-owned Ohio territory by the 1750s. Their quest for new land soon brought them into conflict with France and a war for control of North America.

Indentured servants provided cheap labor to their employers.

# Living in Virginia

Many settlers came to the colony from Europe as **indentured servants** during the 1600s. Indentured servants worked several years in return for an employer paying their way to the colony. The servants were then free to buy their own land to farm. A few became skilled tradesmen who started businesses or worked on plantations. Female indentured servants often got married after they had served their time.

← Possibly half of all white settlers in the early colonies were indentured servants.

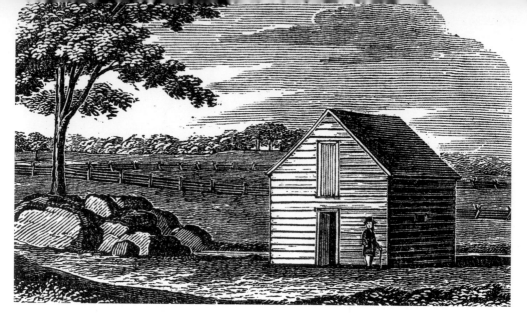

**Farmhouses were often small and simple, especially on the frontier.**

# Plowing and Planting

The first farmers in a region cleared the land of trees and built log cabins to live in. They built wooden houses as the land became more settled. Stone houses were common in German areas. Men worked in the fields plowing the soil and planting crops, such as maize and tobacco. Many families raised pigs and chickens to add meat to the family diet. Frontier men and their sons also hunted deer, rabbit, and squirrel.

# Women at Work

Women on a farm cared for small children, prepared food, made and mended clothes, and tended gardens. Virginia had few doctors. Women usually cared for the sick and injured with remedies they made from herbs, roots, and bark. Frontier women also learned how to handle firearms. They sometimes had to use the guns during attacks by Native Americans or wild animals.

Some colonial women were married by the time they were 14 years old.

**Women protected their homes when men were away.**

# Childhood

Children of wealthy plantation owners often had private teachers. But children on small farms and frontier farms rarely learned reading and writing unless taught by one of their parents. Children spent their time helping with the long list of chores necessary to run the farm. They sometimes played with other children at gatherings with nearby farm families.

**Colonial parents relied on their children to help with chores.**

Between 1640 and 1704, the number of black slaves in Virginia grew from about 150 to 10,000.

**Slavery became a major part of Virginia's economy during the 17th century.**

## Slave Life

Virginians began to use slave labor in 1619. These first slaves were brought by the Dutch from Africa. Many did not remain enslaved for life. They were given tools and land along with their freedom after a period of time. The system changed as English ships brought enslaved Africans to Virginia. Laws made these people slaves for their entire lives. An owner could mistreat them or sell them for any reason. The children of enslaved people were also enslaved.

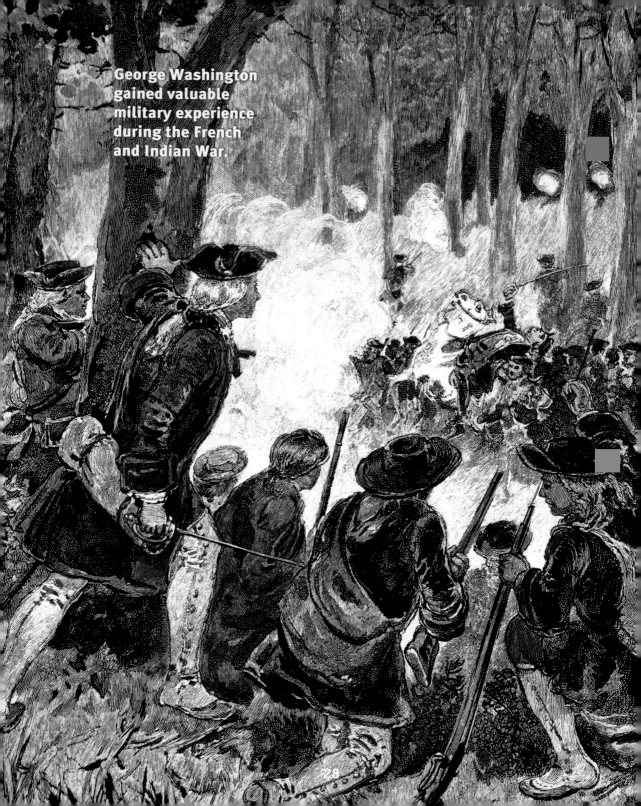

George Washington gained valuable military experience during the French and Indian War.

# CHAPTER 4

# The Road to Revolution

Virginia settlers began to push into the Ohio River valley in the 1740s. France had already claimed the area. But Great Britain also wanted it. A young George Washington led a force of Virginia **militia** into the area near present-day Pittsburgh to stop the French from building forts in 1754. Their battles with French soldiers and their Native American **allies** began the French and Indian War. This war was also called the Seven Years' War.

← The French and Indian War was part of a larger war that was also fought in Europe.

**The colonists often treated tax collectors poorly.**

# The Cost of Victory

The Virginia militia served with British troops during the war. The British and colonial troops defeated France in 1760. They had help from Native American allies. A peace treaty was signed three years later. The long war forced the British to borrow huge amounts of money to pay for soldiers and forts. Britain's legislature, Parliament, imposed taxes on the American colonists to raise money.

# "Taxation Without Representation"

A tax on sugar and other products was unpopular. But the Stamp Act of 1765 angered the colonists. The act forced them to buy stamps for printed materials, such as newspapers and legal documents. Colonists paid taxes to their colonial governments. But they elected the legislatures that had passed those laws. They had no representatives in Parliament to argue for their rights or against taxes. Colonists began to complain about "taxation without representation."

**Many colonists protested the Stamp Act by burning stamps.**

Stamps were a common form of taxation in Great Britain.

Patrick Henry was a member of Virginia's House of Burgesses. He led an effort to declare that colonists could only be taxed by their own representatives. Virginia's governor was a British official. He answered by closing the House of Burgesses. Protests and a **boycott** against British goods convinced Parliament to end the Stamp Act in early 1766. The British passed new taxes. But they cancelled most of them as protests and boycotts continued.

Patrick Henry later became known for saying "Give me liberty or give me death!"

# Tea and Patriots

The only remaining tax by the 1770s was on tea. But tea was the most popular drink in the colonies. Many colonists protested by refusing to buy British tea. Parliament then allowed a British company to sell its tea without paying the tax. But American companies still had to pay it. A group of angry **Patriots** in Boston reacted by dumping British tea into the harbor. The event became known as the Boston Tea Party.

**Patriots disguised themselves as American Indians during the Boston Tea Party.**

# The War Begins

On September 5, 1774, **delegates** from 12 colonies met at the First Continental Congress in Philadelphia to discuss the situation. Very few of those present wanted independence from Britain. They instead wrote King George III asking for fairer treatment. The king ignored them. Massachusetts militia and British soldiers fought at Lexington and Concord one month before a Second Continental Congress was due to meet in 1775. The clash marked the start of the American Revolutionary War.

**The Continental Congress was the earliest form of national government in the colonies.**

There were 56 representatives at the First Continental Congress.

**Continental soldiers did not have the equipment or training of the British military.**

George Washington was chosen to lead the newly formed Continental army. The army lacked uniforms and weapons. It had to steal most of its gunpowder from the British. British troops and their German allies were professional soldiers. Washington had to rely on colonial militias that included farmers, tradesmen, and even members of the congress.

# Virginia's Founding Fathers

Virginia broke away from Britain by declaring itself an independent commonwealth in June 1776. Its **constitution** included a Declaration of Rights. This declaration was written by plantation owner George Mason. The document stated that all men were equal. It also promised religious freedom and freedom of the press. Fellow Virginian Thomas Jefferson borrowed some of Mason's ideas when writing the Declaration of Independence. The Second Continental Congress approved Jefferson's declaration on July 2, 1776. Seven Virginians, including these three men, signed the document.

# Benjamin Harrison

Benjamin Harrison was a plantation owner. He served in the House of Burgesses before being chosen for the Continental Congress. He served three years as Virginia's governor after the war. His son William and great-grandson Benjamin each became president of the United States.

# Thomas Nelson Jr.

Thomas Nelson, Jr., had spent time in the House of Burgesses before the war. Nelson served as the Virginia militia's first commander during the war. He led Virginian troops at the Battle of Yorktown while also acting as the state's governor.

# George Wythe

George Wythe was a well-known lawyer who helped create Virginia's state government. He was unable to sign the Declaration at the same time as his fellow Virginians. The other delegates instead saved a space above their names so that, when Wythe finally signed it, his name would appear first. He later argued against slavery and freed his family's slaves.

Few battles took place on Virginia's soil in the war's early years except for small clashes between Patriots and pro-British **Loyalists**. But Virginians served in both the state militia and Continental army. British troops finally arrived in Virginia at the end of 1780. They were led by Benedict Arnold. Arnold was once an American general. Their raids destroyed valuable storehouses and metalworking factories. Arnold was a traitor to the American cause for independence. He took control of Richmond.

**Patriots clashed with British Loyalists during the revolution.**

About one-third of all colonists remained loyal to Great Britain during the revolution.

# Thomas Jefferson

Thomas Jefferson was one of the most important figures in U.S. history. He was born into a slave-owning plantation family in Virginia in 1743. He studied law and became a better writer than he was a speaker. The Second Continental Congress asked the 33-year-old Jefferson to write the Declaration of Independence. Jefferson believed that his greatest work was not the Declaration, but Virginia's Statute of Religious Freedom. It was written in 1786. The document promised freedom of worship in that state.

# Fighting in Virginia

Virginia's militia and Continental soldiers chased Arnold back to the coast. But they faced a second force of British soldiers in the spring of 1781. British general Charles Cornwallis invaded Virginia with a large but battered army. He hoped to receive supplies and new troops from the British navy at Yorktown. The Continental army and the French navy cornered him there. Cornwallis surrendered after a three-week **siege**. Parliament ended the war.

About 8,000 British soldiers were taken prisoner during the Siege of Yorktown.

**Cornwallis surrendered to General Washington on October 19, 1781.**

# After the War

The former colonies had won their independence. But it would take time to rebuild. Thousands of Virginians had died. Entire towns lay in ruins. The people of Virginia had lost years of tobacco profits. The British had also freed thousands of slaves. This created a shortage of workers. Benjamin Harrison and Patrick Henry would lead Virginia in the difficult first years after the war.

**Today, a statue of Patrick Henry stands at the Virginia state capital.**

# New State, New Nation

Americans wrestled with the idea of creating a stronger national government as the 1780s continued. Delegates from 12 states met in 1787 to write a constitution for the nation. The U.S. Constitution then went to each state for approval. Virginia refused to approve it until the delegates added a Bill of Rights promising freedoms like those in the Virginia Declaration of Rights. Virginia approved the Constitution on June 25, 1788. It became the 10th state in the Union. ★

Virginia's Declaration of Rights was the model for the Bill of Rights.

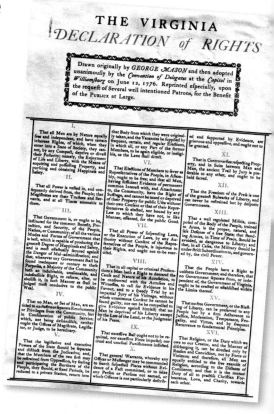

THE VIRGINIA DECLARATION of RIGHTS

Drawn originally by *GEORGE MASON* and then adopted unanimously by the *Convention of Delegates* at the *Capitol* in *Williamsburg* on June 12, 1776. Reprinted especially, upon the request of several well intentioned Patrons, for the Benefit of the PUBLICK at Large.

# True Statistics

**Number of original settlers at Jamestown:** 104

**Year John Smith met Pocahontas:** 1607

**Amount of tobacco sent from Jamestown to England in 1616:** 2,500 lbs. (1,135 kg)

**Percentage of early Jamestown colonists who died soon after arrival:** 80 percent

**Length of service for an indentured servant:** 7 years

**Number of representatives in the first House of Burgesses:** 22

**Number of slaves in Virginia in 1730:** 28,500

**Number of slaves in Virginia in 1790:** 292,627

**Number of Virginians who signed the Declaration of Independence:** 7

**Number of U.S. presidents born in Virginia:** 8

## Did you find the truth?

**(T)** George Washington fought in the French and Indian War.

**(F)** Jamestown was a successful colony from its beginning.

# Resources

## Books

Bauer, Brandy. *The Virginia Colony*. Mankato, MN: Capstone, 2006.

DeAngelis, Gina. *Virginia*. New York: Children's Press, 2001.

Doak, Robin S. *John Smith and the Settlement of Jamestown*. Mankato, MN: Compass Point, 2003.

Fradin, Dennis B. *Jamestown, Virginia*. New York: Benchmark, 2007.

Harkins, Susan Sales, and William H. Harkins. *Colonial Virginia*. Hockessin, DE: Mitchell Lane, 2008.

King, David C. *The Powhatan*. New York: Benchmark, 2008.

Lange, Karen E. *1607: A New Look at Jamestown*. Washington, DC: National Geographic, 2007.

Marsh, Carole. *Jamestown*. Peachtree City, GA: Gallopade International, 2006.

# Organizations and Web Sites

## Preservation Virginia: Historic Jamestowne

http://historicjamestowne.org
See what archaeologists have dug up recently at the site of the Jamestown settlement.

## Virginia Historical Society

www.vahistorical.org
View online exhibits on a number of topics covering Virginia history from the time of the Powhatan to the present.

# Places to Visit

## Monticello

931 Thomas Jefferson Parkway
Charlottesville, VA 22902
(434) 984-9822
www.monticello.org
Explore Thomas Jefferson's 5,000-acre (2,025 hectare) plantation and historic house.

## Mount Vernon

3200 Mount Vernon Memorial Highway
Mount Vernon, VA 22309
(800) 429-1520
www.mountvernon.org
Tour George Washington's home and estate, and enjoy many other activities.

# Important Words

**allies** (AL-eyes)—people or countries that are on the same side during a war or disagreement

**boycott** (BOI-kaht)— act of refusing to buy goods from a person, group, or country

**confederacy** (kuhn-FED-ur-uh-see)—a number of groups or countries that gather together to help one another

**constitution** (kahn-sti-TOO-shun)—the laws of a country that state the rights of the people and the powers of government

**delegates** (DEL-i-gitz)—representatives to a convention or congress

**indentured servants** (in-DEHN-shurd SUR-vents)—people who agreed to work a certain amount of time in return for paid transportation to the colonies

**legislature** (LEJ-is-lay-chur)—a body with the power to make or change laws

**Loyalists** (LOI-uhl-ists)—American colonists who remained faithful to Great Britain

**militia** (muh-LISH-uh)—a group of people who are trained to fight but who aren't professional soldiers

**Patriots** (PAY-tree-uhts)—American colonists opposed to rule by Great Britain

**siege** (SEEJ)—the surrounding of a place to cut off supplies

# Index

Page numbers in **bold** indicate illustrations

# About the Author

Kevin Cunningham has written more than 40 books on disasters, the history of disease, Native Americans, and other topics. Cunningham lives near Chicago with his wife and young daughter.